THE LAUGH OUT LOUD CRAZY JOKE BOOK

ARCTURUS

This edition published in 2013 by Arcturus Publishing Limited
26/27 Bickels Yard, 151–153 Bermondsey Street,
London SE1 3HA

ISBN: 978-1-78212-293-7
CH003608EN
Supplier 05 Date 0713, Print Run 2460

Written by Sean Connolly
Edited by Joe Harris and Samantha Noonan
Illustration by Adam Clay and Dynamo Limited
Design by Notion Design and Debbie Fisher

Printed in Singapore

CONTENTS

Welcome to The Laugh Out Loud Crazy Joke Book!

Get ready to giggle and snigger your way through six hilarious chapters of jokes and gags! From bonkers bunnies to ridiculous robots, this book takes you around the world, under the sea and back in time, tickling your funny bone all the way! Your family and friends will love this fantastic collection - so dive in and get ready to laugh out loud!

JOLLY JUNGLE

Why should you never trust a giraffe?
They are always telling tall stories.

What do elephants take to help them sleep?
Trunkquilizers!

What flies through the jungle singing opera?
The Parrots of Penzance.

Teacher: What do you think a pair of alligator shoes would cost?
Pupil: That would depend on the size of your alligator's feet!

Why do elephants paint their toenails red?
So they can hide in cherry trees!

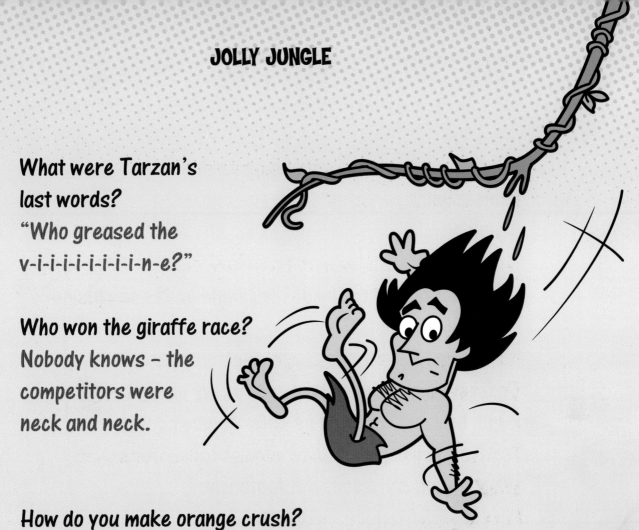

What were Tarzan's
last words?
"Who greased the
v-i-i-i-i-i-i-i-n-e?"

Who won the giraffe race?
Nobody knows – the
competitors were
neck and neck.

How do you make orange crush?
Get an elephant to jump up and down in the fruit and
vegetable aisle!

How do hippos commute?
By hippopotabus.

Teacher: Define "polygon".
Pupil: A missing parrot!

What sort of dancing will elephants do in your
front room?
Break dancing!

Why can't I get the king of the jungle on the telephone?
Because the lion is busy!

Teacher: Have you written your essay on big cats?
Pupil: I thought it would be safer to use paper!

What do you call a lion with toothache?
Rory!

What do you call a hippo
that always claims to be sick?
A hippochondriac.

Why did the firefly
keep crashing?
He wasn't very
bright.

What did King
Kong say when
he was told that
his sister had
had a baby?
"Well, I'll be a
monkey's uncle!"

What do you call a show
full of lions?
The mane event.

What do you get if you cross a parrot with a snake?
A feather boa.

Who is in charge of the stick insects?
The branch manager!

Knock, knock!
Who's there?
Orange!
Orange who?
Orange you glad to see me?

Spotted in the jungle library:
Why Giant Snails Get Tired by Michelle Sevy

Baby snake: Dad, are we poisonous?
Dad snake: No, son, why do you ask?
Baby snake: I've just bitten my tongue!

What do you call an alligator private eye?
An investi-gator.

What do you get if you cross a tarantula with a rose?
We're not sure, but don't try smelling it!

Why don't bananas sunbathe?
Because they would peel.

What happens if you cross a hummingbird with a doorbell?
You get a humdinger.

What does the lemur do every evening?
He curls up with his best-loved tail.

What do you call a lion with no eyes?
Lon!

Why does a frog have more lives than a cat?
Because it croaks every night.

How do you fix a broken chimp?
With a monkey wrench!

What's orange and sounds like a parrot?
A carrot.

Is it hard to spot a leopard?
Not at all – they come that way!

What do toucans sing at Christmas?
Jungle Bells.

What advice did the parrot give to the toucan?
Talk is cheep.

What do monkeys wear when they cook?
Ape-rons.

How did the monkey get down the stairs?
It slid down the banana-ster.

What did the snake give his date when he dropped her off?
He gave her a goodnight hiss.

Why did the leopard refuse to take a bath?
Because he didn't
want to become
spotless.

What language do oranges speak?
Mandarin.

Why should you never tell a giraffe a secret?
Because you could fall off his neck as you whisper in his ear.

What did Tarzan tell his son?
"Be careful – it's a jungle out there."

What's sweet and crunchy and swings through the trees?
A meringue-utan.

What's worse than a crocodile with a toothache?
A centipede with athlete's foot.

What ice-cream does
a gorilla like best?
Chocolate chimp.

Why do giraffes have
small appetites?
Because a little goes a long way.

What is hairy and orange and always comes back to you?
A boomerang-utan.

What happens if you upset a cannibal?
You get into hot water.

What do you get if you cross a gorilla with a porcupine?
A seat on the bus!

Which animals were the last to leave Noah's Ark?
The elephants – they had to pack their trunks.

What do you give a gorilla that's going to throw up?
Plenty of room!

What happens if you cross an elephant and a canary?
You get a very messy cage.

What class do snakes like best at school?
Hissssstory.

What's the most dangerous animal in your backyard?
The clothes-lion.

What do you call an exploding ape?
A ba-BOOM!

What did the banana say to the gorilla?
Nothing, bananas can't talk!

What do you get if you cross a snake with a pig?
A boar constrictor.

What do you get when you cross an elephant with a kangaroo?
Big holes all over Australia.

Why did the leopard eat the tightrope walker?
He wanted a balanced diet.

Why do elephants never forget?
Because no one ever tells them anything.

What's the best time to buy parakeets?
When they're going cheep.

Why are anteaters so healthy?
Because they're full of anty-bodies.

Why does Tarzan shout so loudly?
Because it hurts when he pounds his chest.

What do you call two rhinos on a bicycle?
Optimistic.

Teacher: They say time flies like an arrow.
Pupil: Yes, but fruit flies like a banana.

What would you get if a python slipped into a tuba?
A snake in the brass.

What has 99 legs and one eye?
A pirate centipede.

What has three trunks, two tails, and six feet?
An elephant with spare parts.

Why couldn't the butterfly go to the dance?
Because it was a moth ball.

What did the boa constrictor say to his girlfriend?
"I have a crush on you!"

What do you get if you cross a parrot with a shark?
A bird that will talk your ear off.

What did the bee say when it returned to the hive?
"Honey, I'm home."

What happened to the cannibal lion?
He had to swallow his pride.

What should you do if a rhino charges you?
Pay him!

How did the rival apes settle their differences?
With a gorilla war.

What do you get if you cross an elephant with a parrot?
An animal that tells you everything it remembers.

What's black and white and red all over?
A zebra with a sunburn.

Why did the canary refuse to work in a coal mine?
He said it was beneath him.

What did the tiger say when he cut off his tail?
It won't be long now.

What's the medical term for memory loss in parrots?
Polynesia.

What line of work did the parrot take up after it swallowed a clock?
Politics.

What do you call a rabbit that can beat up a lion?
Sir.

Why should you value an elephant's opinion?
Because it carries a lot of weight.

What do you call a snail on a turtle's shell?
A thrill seeker.

Why did the monkey take a banana to the doctor's?
Because it wasn't peeling well.

How do you start a firefly race?
By saying "On your marks, get set, glow!"

What do wasps do when they build a new nest?
They have a house-swarming party.

Knock, knock!
Who's there?
Cash!
Cash who?
**No thanks, but
I'd love a peanut!**

**Why did
Tarzan spend
so much time on
the golf course?**
He was perfecting
his swing.

**What do you call a
failed lion tamer?**
Claude Behind!

**Why don't farmers grow bananas
any longer?**
Because they're long enough already.

How does the vet check the tiger's teeth for cavities?
Very carefully!

How do you measure a cobra?
In inches – they don't have any feet.

First man: I took my son to the zoo last week.
Second man: Really? And which cage is he in now?

SILLY SPELLS

**What happens when
a witch on a broomstick
brakes too hard?**
She flies off the handle.

How do witches tell the time?
With witch watches.

**Where does the wizards' school store its
weightlifting equipment?**
Behind the dumbbell door.

How do elves greet each other?
"Small world, isn't it?"

How do Jamaican ghosts style their hair?
In deadlocks!

What happened to the witch who swallowed a poisonous toad?
She croaked!

What do you call a witch's garage?
A broom closet.

Who scared the troll under the bridge?
The billy ghosts Gruff.

Which jokes go down well with skeletons?
Rib ticklers!

Who said, "Get lost," to the Big Bad Wolf?
Little Rude Riding Hood.

What is a wizzerd?
A wizard who can't spell!

Knock, knock!
Who's there?
Al.
Al who?
Al huff and I'll puff and blow your house down!

What do you get if you cross a skeleton and a garden spade?
Skullduggery!

What kind of shoes do witches wear in the summer?
Open toad sandals!

Where do you find monster snails?
On the end of monsters' fingers!

What do you call
a fairy that has
never taken a
bath?
Stinkerbell!

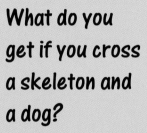

What do you
get if you cross
a skeleton and
a dog?
An animal that buries itself!

Who's that at the door?
The invisible man.
Tell him I can't see him.

What did the headless ghost get when he fell through a
window?
A pane in the neck!

What do witches sing at Christmas?
Deck the Halls with Poison Ivy.

SiLLY SPELLS

Why did the pixie move out of the toadstool?
Because there wasn't mushroom.

Why is Frankenstein's monster bad at school?
He doesn't have the brains he was born with!

Baby ogre: When I grow up, I want to drive a tank!
Mommy ogre: Well, I certainly won't stand in your way!

How many guests has the zombie invited to his party?
It depends on who he could dig up!

What do monster children do on Halloween?
They go from door to door dressed as humans!

SILLY SPELLS

What's big, red, and eats rocks?
A big, red rock-eater!

What do ghostly police officers do?
They haunt down criminals!

Why don't giants speak to leprechauns?
They're no good at small talk.

Did you hear about the incredibly clever monster?
He was called Frank Einstein.

What do you call
two witches who
live together?
Broommates!

SILLY SPELLS

What do Italian ghosts eat for dinner?
Spookhetti!

What did the monster say to the scruffy werewolf?
"You look like you're going to the dogs!"

Why couldn't the wizard move?
He was spellbound!

Why was the skeleton's jacket in shreds?
Because he had very sharp shoulder blades!

Why would Snow White be a good judge?
Because she is the fairest in the land.

Where do you normally find elves?
It depends where you left them!

Which fairy-tale creature has the most teeth?
A dragon?
No, the tooth fairy!

Why did the headless ghost go to the psychiatrist?
Because he wasn't all there!

What did the No Parking sign outside the witch's house say?
Violators will be toads!

How do two ghosts decide who owns something?
They fright each other for it!

SILLY SPELLS

What type of
spells did the
whirling wizard cast?
Dizzy spells.

What goes cackle,
squelch, cackle,
squelch?
A witch in soggy
tennis shoes.

What noise does a
witch's car make?
Broom, broom!

What do you call a vampire that hides in the kitchen?
Spatula!

What do you call a magician's assistant?
Magic Trixie!

SILLY SPELLS

Why didn't the witch sing a solo at the concert?
Because she had a frog in her throat.

Why was the ogre catching centipedes?
He wanted scrambled legs for breakfast!

Where would you find a suitable gift for a tortured ghost?
In a chain store!

What did the police do to the giant who ran away with the circus?
They made him bring it back.

Which great detective is three feet tall and has pointed ears?
Sherlock Gnomes.

SILLY SPELLS

Did you hear about the vampire who fell asleep in the wrong coffin?
It was a grave mistake!

What happened to the boxer who got knocked out by Dracula?
He was out for the Count.

Knock, knock.
Who's there?
Aladdin.
Aladdin who?
Aladdin the street who wants to come in!

What is the difference between
a dragon and a mouse?
Have you had your eyes
tested recently?

Why can't you borrow money from a leprechaun?
Because he's always a little short.

Who lights up a haunted house?
The lights witch.

What did the big candle say to the little candle?
I'm going out tonight.

Did you hear about the tiny, winged Egyptian king?
He was a fairy pharaoh!

How do you fix a jack-o'-lantern?
Use a pumpkin patch.

SILLY SPELLS

Why did the head druid keep falling over?
He couldn't get the staff.

What do you call a wizard who's really good at golf?
Harry Putter.

What do demons pack for their picnics?
Deviled eggs.

Why did the witch put her broom in the wash?
She wanted a clean sweep.

What do you call a warlock who tries to stop fights?
A peacelock.

Why are mermaids easy to weigh?
Because they have their own scales.

What does Medusa do on a bad hair day?
She pays a visit to the snake charmer.

Why was the giant's hand only eleven inches long?
An inch longer, and it would be a foot.

What do you call a female wizard?
Magic Wanda.

When do ghosts usually appear?
Just before somebody screams.

Why was Cinderella a terrible tennis player?
She kept running away from the ball.

How do you make a witch itch?
Take away the "w"!

When I grow up, I'd like to marry a ghost.
What would possess you to do that?

How did the Good Weather Wizard get his name?
He loved sunny spells.

How can you tell whether a leprechaun is enjoying himself?
He's Dublin over with laughter.

What parting gift was the young werewolf given when he left home?
A comb!

What's the definition of "Deadline"?
A fence around a graveyard!

Why do dragons sleep all day?
So they can fight knights!

What do you call a big, fat troll?
A wobblin' goblin.

What do you call a wizard with a cold?
A blizzard.

Why do witches have painful joints?
They get broomatism.

Why did the ogre's mother knit him three socks as a birthday present?
Because he had grown another foot.

What does the witch use to keep her doors secure?
Warlocks!

What did the giant police officer eat for lunch?
Beef burglars!

Why did Jack Frost refuse to get married?
Because he got cold feet!

Who grants your
wishes but smells
of fishes?
The fairy
cod-mother.

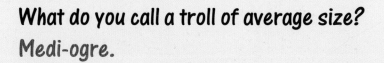

Why did the
dragon breathe
on the map of
the Earth?
Because he
wanted to set the world on fire.

What do you call a troll of average size?
Medi-ogre.

What happened to the man who didn't pay the exorcist's
bill on time?
He was repossessed.

What does a witch doctor ask his guests at the start of
a meal?
"Voodoo like to sit down?"

Which fairy-tale character has a black belt in kung fu?
The ninja bread man.

What is a female elf called?
A shelf.

What is the first thing an ogre does when you give him a knife?
He writes out a chopping list!

What do you call a man who rescues drowning phantoms from the sea?
A Ghost Guard.

What happened to the witch with the gingerbread house?
She was eaten out of house and home!

HYSTERICAL HISTORY

When did early people start wearing uncreased clothes? In the Iron Age!

What did Robin Hood wear to the Sherwood Forest ball? A bow tie.

What was the moral of the story of Jonah and the whale? You can't keep a good man down!

Teacher: Can you name a fierce warrior king?
Pupil: King Kong?

What sort of music did cavemen enjoy?
Rock music!

Teacher: Name an ancient musical instrument.
Pupil: An Anglo-saxophone?

What should you do if you see a caveman?
Go inside and explore, man!

What was Noah's job?
He was an ark-itect.

Why were undertakers in ancient Egypt such successful detectives?
They were good at wrapping up their cases.

What's purple and 5,000 miles long?
The grape wall of China.

Teacher: Surely you can remember what happened in 1776?
Pupil: It's all right for you – you were there!

Who was the fastest runner of all time?
Adam, because he was first in the human race!

Why did the king go to the dentist?
To get his teeth crowned.

Why did the student miss history class?
He had the wrong date.

Why was England so wet in the nineteenth century? Because Queen Victoria's reign lasted 64 years.

Which ancient leader invented seasonings?
Sultan Pepper!

Who succeeded the first President of the United States?
The second one.

Why did the very first fries not taste very nice?
Because they were fried in ancient Greece!

Teacher: Can you name a famous religious warrior?
Pupil: Attila the Nun!

Teacher: Where would you find a cowboy?
Pupil: In a field – and stop calling me "boy"!

What music do Egyptian mummies like best?
Wrap music!

What do you call the Roman Emperor who kept pet mice?
Julius Cheeser!

How did Moses cut the sea in half?
With a sea-saw.

Teacher: How did knights make chain mail?
Pupil: From steel wool?

Who built the Ark?
I have Noah idea.

Where were French traitors beheaded?
Just above the shoulders!

Two wrongs don't make a right, but what do two rights make?
The first airplane!

Teacher: Why did Robin Hood steal from the rich?
Pupil: Because the poor didn't have anything worth stealing!

Teacher: How did the Dark Ages get their name?
Pupil: Because there were so many knights!

First Roman soldier: What's the time?
Second Roman soldier: XV past VIII.
First Roman soldier:
By the time I work
that out, it will
be midnight!

What is an archeologist?
Someone whose career is in ruins.

What do you call the king who invented the fireplace?
Alfred the Grate!

What did King Henry VIII do whenever he burped?
He issued a royal pardon.

Where was the Declaration of Independence signed?
At the bottom.

How did Vikings send secret messages?
By Norse code.

Which emperor should never have played with explosives?
Napoleon Blownapart!

Why do historians believe that Rome was built at night?
Because it wasn't built in a day.

In which battle was Alexander the Great killed?
His last one!

Where did Viking teachers send sick children?
To the school Norse.

What was King John's castle famous for?
Its knight life.

Which historical character was always eating?
Attila the Hungry!

What did Robin Hood say when he was almost hit at the archery tournament?
"That was an arrow escape!"

Teacher: Today we're studying ancient Rome. Can anyone tell me what a forum was?
Pupil: A two-um plus a two-um?

What did Attila's wife say to get his attention?
"Over here, Hun."

What did the caveman give his girlfriend on Valentine's Day?
Ugs and kisses.

Why did King Arthur have a Round Table?
So that no one could corner him.

What do Alexander the Great and Billy the Kid have in common?
The same middle name.

How do we know that the ancient Romans had an expensive education?
Because they could all speak Latin.

Why couldn't the mummy answer the phone?
He was too wrapped up!

Who would referee a tennis match between Julius Caesar and Brutus?
A Roman umpire.

Who sailed on the ghost ship?
The skeleton crew.

Did prehistoric people hunt bear?
No – they wore clothes!

Why did the mammoth have a woolly coat?
Because it would have looked silly in a parka.

What was written on the knight's tomb?
"May he rust in peace."

What snack did the
caveman like best?
A club sandwich.

Which king had the largest crown?
The one with the biggest head!

Teacher: What came after the Stone Age and the Bronze Age?
Pupil: The sausage?

In which era did people sunbathe the most?
The Bronzed Age.

What did the ancient Egyptians call bad leaders?
Un-Pharaohs.

What happened to the knight who lost his left arm and left leg in battle?
He was all right in the end.

Where do Egyptian mummies go for a swim?
To the Dead Sea.

How did Columbus's men sleep on the boat?
With their eyes shut.

Why did Eve move to New York?
She fell for the Big Apple.

What do you call a blind dinosaur?
Doyouthinkhesaurus.

What has two eyes, two legs and two noses?
Two pirates!

What did the executioner say to the former king?
It's time to head off!

Why did the mammoth have a trunk?
Because it would have looked silly with suitcases.

What do you call a pyramid overlooking the Nile?
A tomb with a view.

What did the cowboy say when he saw a cow in a tree?
Howdy get there?

Which Egyptian pharaoh played the trumpet?
Tootin' Kamun.

What do history teachers talk about when they get together?

The good old days.

What do you call a prehistoric monster when it is asleep?

A dino-snore.

Why did Columbus cross the ocean?

To get to the other tide.

Who made dinner for Robin Hood and his Merry Men?

Frier Tuck

Which knight designed King Arthur's Round Table!

Sir Cumference!

What was the first thing Queen Elizabeth I did when she ascended the throne?
She sat down.

Pupil: I wish I had been born 1,000 years ago.
Teacher: Why is that?
Pupil: Because I wouldn't have had to learn so much history!

How did the Roman cannibal feel about his mother-in-law?
Gladiator.

What was the most popular movie in ancient Greece?
Troy Story.

What happened when the wheel was invented?
It caused a revolution.

Did Adam and Eve ever have a date?
No, but they had an apple!

Where was the Ink-an Empire?
In Pen-sylvania.

How was the Roman Empire cut in half?
With a pair of Caesars.

Where did Napoleon keep his armies?
Up his sleevies.

Why did the court jester swallow fire?
Because he wanted to burn some calories.

What happened when electricity was discovered?
Someone got a nasty shock.

Why did the nervous knight withdraw from the archery contest?
It was an arrowing experience.

How did Robin Hood tie his bootlaces?
With a long bow.

What did Thomas Edison's mother say when he showed her the electric light he had invented?
"That's wonderful, dear. Now turn it off and go to bed."

Why did the Romans build straight roads?
So the soldiers didn't go round the bend.

What did Mount Vesuvius say to Pompeii?
I lava you.

What do you call an archeologist that sleeps all the time?
Lazy bones.

Which protest by a group of cats and dogs took place
in 1773?
The Boston Flea Party.

Why did Captain Cook sail to Australia?
It was too far to swim.

What did Columbus do after
he crossed the Atlantic?
He dried his clothes.

Why did Cleopatra take milk baths?
She couldn't find a cow tall enough for her to take a shower.

Which Viking explorer had a greenhouse on his longboat?
Leaf Eriksson.

Why did the T. rex wear a bandage?
He had a dino-sore!

What do you call George Washington's false teeth?
Presi-dentures.

Which pirate told the most jokes?
Captain Kidd.

Why did the pioneers cross America in covered wagons? Because they didn't want to wait thirty years for the first train.

Why was Charlemagne able to draw such straight lines?
He was a good ruler.

What did Noah use to find his way in the dark?
Floodlights.

What king invented fractions?
King Henry the $\frac{1}{8}$th.

Why were the first European settlers in America like ants?
Because they lived in colonies.

CRAZY COMPUTERS

What do you call a flying printer?
An inkjet!

Spotted in the library:
How to Build a Shrink Ray by Minnie Mize

Where is the world's biggest computer?
In New York – it's the Big Apple!

Which cartoon character do robots like best?
Tin-tin!

Why did the medical computer go to prison?
It had performed an illegal operation.

Where does the biggest spider in the universe live? On the World Wide Web.

What do you call a man with a speedometer in the middle of his forehead? Miles!

How do computers say goodbye?
"See you later, calculator!"

Teacher: Steven, what's a computer byte?
Pupil: I didn't even know they had teeth!

What do you get if you cross a computer with a lifeguard?
A screensaver.

CRAZY COMPUTERS

Why are birds always on the Internet?
They just love tweeting.

What was the robot doing at the gym?
Pumping iron.

Why did the robot boxer sit on the stove before the big match?
He wanted to strike while the iron was hot.

Which cookie do computers like best?
Chocolate microchip.

If human babies are delivered by stork, how are
robot babies delivered?
By crane!

CRAZY COMPUTERS

What did the computer nerd say when his mother opened the curtains?
Wow, look at those graphics!

Why are evil robots so shiny?
Because there's no rust for the wicked.

Did you hear about the kid who had his ID stolen?
Now he's just a "k".

Spotted in the library:
Robots Are People Too by Anne Droid.

What happened to the robot
who put his shoes on the wrong feet?
He had to be rebooted.

What's orange and points North?
A magnetic carrot.

First robot: Are you enjoying that book about magnetism?
Second robot: Yes, I can't put it down!

Why was the thirsty astronaut hanging out near the computer keyboard?
He was looking for the space bar.

Did you hear about the couple who adopted a calculator?
It made a great addition to the family.

Why did the Apple Mac programmer live in the dark?
Because he refused to use Windows.

Why did the boy bring a surfboard to school?
The teacher said they were going to be surfing the Internet.

Why was the computer such a terrific golfer?
It had a hard drive.

How do lumberjacks get on the Internet?
They log on.

What do you call a man with a cable coming out of his ear?
Mike!

What do you buy for someone who already has all the latest gadgets?
A burglar alarm.

Why did the robot get angry?
Someone kept pushing his buttons!

What do you get if you cross a large computer and a hamburger?
A Big Mac!

Why do robots never feel queasy?
They have cast iron stomachs.

Why did the pupil fall asleep in computer class?
He was feeling key-bored.

What do you give a robot who feels like a light snack?
Some 60-watt bulbs!

What's the difference between computer hardware and software?
Hardware is the stuff that you can kick when it doesn't work.

What goes in one year and out the other?
A time machine!

Teacher: Give me an example of cutting edge technology.
Pupil: A pair of scissors?

My computer is powered by clockwork.
Really?
No, I was just winding you up.

What music do robots like to listen to?
Heavy metal!

CRAZY COMPUTERS

How can you tell if a robot is happy to see you?
Because his eyes light up.

What do you get from robot sheep?
Steel wool.

Why did the computer programmer give up his job?
He lost his drive.

Why was the electrified robot so badly behaved?
It didn't know how to conduct itself.

Did you hear about the robot dog?
His megabark was worse than his megabyte.

CRAZY COMPUTERS

What do you call a robot who turns into a tractor?
A trans-farmer!

Where do cool
mice live?
In mouse pads.

Did you know that
my computer can do
the gardening?
Can it really?
Yes, it's made
with cutting
hedge technology.

Which city has no people?
Electricity.

Did you hear about the two TVs who got married?
Their reception was excellent.

CRAZY COMPUTERS

Why did the boy and girl robots call things off after their first date?
There was no spark.

Why did the robot kiss his girlfriend?
He just couldn't resistor.

How did the inventor of the jetpack feel?
He was on cloud nine!

Why did the storekeeper refuse to serve italic fonts?
He didn't like their type.

Where did the tightrope walker meet his girlfriend?
Online.

CRAZY COMPUTERS

How do snowmen get online?
They use the Winternet.

How does a tiny robot say goodbye?
With a micro-wave.

Brad: Have you seen my high-tech watch belt?
Suzie: It sounds like a waist of time.

Why did the witch buy a computer?
She needed a spell-checker!

What do
astronauts
eat out of?
Satellite
dishes.

How many ears does a robot have?
Three: a left ear, a right ear, and just in case they go wrong, an engine-ear.

What was wrong with the robot shepherd?
He didn't have enough RAM.

What do you call a man with a car on his head?
Jack!

Why was the boy happy when he hurt his eye?
Because the doctor gave him an iPad.

Why did the inventor stuff herbs in the disk drive of his computer?
He was trying to build a thyme machine.

CRAZY COMPUTERS

Why couldn't the computer take its hat off?
Because the caps lock was on.

Spotted in the library:
How to Fix Just About Anything by Andy Mann.

Teacher: Look at the state of the classroom computer. I want that screen cleaned so well I can see my own face in it!
Pupil: But then it will crack!

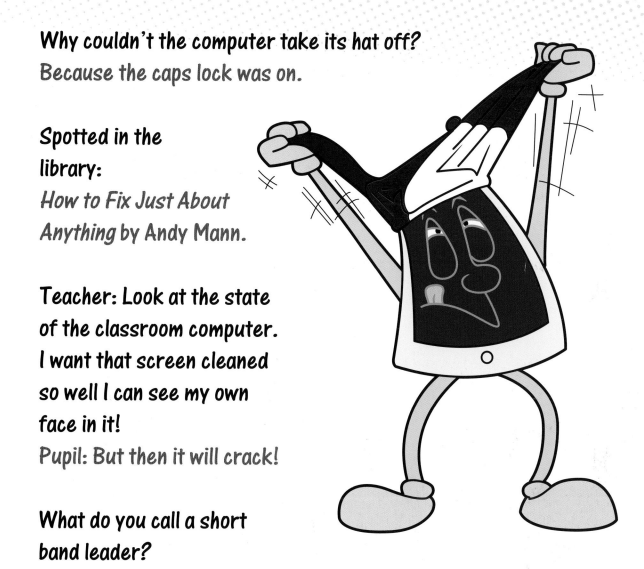

What do you call a short band leader?
A semi-conductor.

Why did the computer catch a cold?
Someone kept leaving its Windows open.

CRAZY COMPUTERS

How did the inventor of the space rocket feel?
Over the moon!

What do you call a robot standing in the rain?
Rusty!

What invention is sillier than glow-in-the-dark sunglasses for midnight sunbathing?
Underwater umbrellas for scuba divers!

Why did the silly girl put her letters in the microwave?
She wanted to use Hotmail.

Why did they have to call off the computer race?
The competitors kept crashing.

CRAZY COMPUTERS

Who won the Oscar for best android actor?
Robot Downey, Jr.

How did the scientist invent insect repellent?
He started from scratch.

There's never anything on TV, is there?
I don't know about that – there's a vase on top of ours.

Have you been on the optician's website?
It's a site for sore eyes.

Why did the computer programmer give up his life of crime?
He couldn't hack it any more.

What do you call a
nervous robot?
A shy-borg.

How do lazy spiders
decorate their
homes?
They hire web
designers.

Do you think
scientists will ever
invent flying
desserts?
No, that's pie in the sky.

What happened when the bossy android charged for
too long?
It went on a power trip!

How did the lazy office worker get his daily exercise?
He turned on his computer and clicked on "run".

CRAZY COMPUTERS

Teacher: Why have you stopped typing?
Pupil: It was making me feel keyed up.

Did you hear about the computer programmer whose illegal activities made him sick?
He gave himself a hacking cough.

Did you have any success with Internet dating?
Yes, it was love at first site.

Why didn't two computers get along?
They got their wires crossed.

What do you call an android with oars?
A row-bot.

What did one calculator say to the other calculator?
You can count on me.

What do robot office workers eat?
A staple diet.

Why did the girl mouse decide not to ask the boy mouse on a second date?
They just didn't click.

Computer repair man: What's wrong with this laptop, sir?
Customer: Thespacebarseemstobestuck.

Have you heard about the new online service for short-sighted people?
It's called the Squinternet.

How do chicks get out of their shells?
They look for the eggs-it.

What's brown and sticky?
A stick!

What do you get if you cross a sheepdog and a fruit?
A melon-collie!

How do you make a chicken stew?
Keep it waiting for a couple of hours.

What do you get when you cross a
rooster with a duck?
A bird that gets
up at the
quack of
dawn.

FUN ON THE FARM

Which ballet do pigs
like best?
Swine Lake.

Teacher: How would
you hire a farm worker?
Pupil: Put a brick under
each leg.

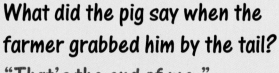

What did the pig say when the
farmer grabbed him by the tail?
"That's the end of me."

Knock, knock!
Who's there?
Farmer.
Farmer who?
Farmer distance, your house looks much bigger!

What happened when the sheep pen broke?
The sheep had to use a pencil.

What's green and sings in the vegetable patch?
Elvis Parsley.

Knock, knock!
Who's there?
Lettuce.
Lettuce who?
Lettuce in and you'll find out!

What did the horse say when it fell over?
"I've fallen and I can't giddy-up."

What do horses tell their children at bedtime?
Pony tales!

Patient: Doctor, what can I do to help me get to sleep?
Doctor: Have you tried counting sheep?
Patient: Yes, but then I have to wake up to drive home again!

What do you give a sick pig?
Oinkment!

How did the musical farmer know which note to sing?
He used a pitchfork!

Why should you be careful where you step when it rains cats and dogs?
You could step in a poodle!

What do you call the wages paid to a gardener?
His celery!

What do you call a sleeping bull?
A bulldozer.

What do you get if you cross a chicken with a kangaroo?
Pouched eggs!

How did the pig with laryngitis feel?
Dis-gruntled.

Why do roosters curse all the time?
They are fowl-mouthed.

What did the waiter say when the horse walked into the café?
Why the long face?

What did the chicken say when it laid a square egg?
Owwww!

What did the flamenco-dancing farmer say to his chickens?
"Oh, lay!"

Patient: Doctor, I feel like a dog!
Doctor: How long have you felt that way?
Patient: Since I was a puppy!

What do you get if you feed gunpowder to a chicken?
An egg-splosion!

Where do horses stay in hotels?
The bridle suite.

What did the farmer use to paint the new sty?
Pigment.

What do you call a factual TV show about sheep?
A flock-umentary!

Why did the goose cross the road?
To prove she wasn't chicken!

Patient: Doctor, I got trampled by a load of cows!
Doctor: So I herd!

What do you give a pony with a cold?
Cough stirrup!

Why should you never tell your secrets to a piglet?
Because they might squeal!

How do alien farmers round up their sheep?
They use tractor beams!

What do you get when you cross a chicken and a fox?
Just the fox.

How can you cook turkey that really tickles the taste buds?
Leave the feathers on!

How many pigs do you need to make a smell?
A phew!

What do you call a cow with an out-of-date map?
Udderly lost!

Where do cows go for history lessons?
To a mooseum!

Which fairy tale do pigs like best?
Slopping Beauty.

If a small duck is called a duckling, what do you call
a small pen?
An inkling!

Mother: You can't keep a pig in your bedroom – what about the terrible smell?
Child: Don't worry, he'll soon get used to it!

What do you get if you cross a donkey and Christmas?
Muletide greetings!

What do you call a dog with a bunch of roses?
A collie-flower!

Why did the farmer's dog keep chasing his tail?
He was trying to make ends meet.

How does a sheep finish a letter?
Sincerely ewes.

Why did the chicken cross the playground?
To get to the other slide!

What sort of jokes do chickens like best?
Corny ones!

What do you get if you cross a cow and a jogging machine?
A milk shake!

Is chicken soup good for your health?
Not if you're the chicken!

What grows down as it grows up?
A goose!

Why is that farmer setting fire to the plants in his field?
He's growing baked beans!

What do you call a man who keeps rabbits?
Warren!

What says, "Moo, baa, woof, quack, meow, oink?"
A sheep that speaks foreign languages!

What do you get if you cross a cow with a camel?
Lumpy milkshakes!

Where do sheep get shorn?
At the baa-baas!

What has lots of ears, but can't hear anything at all?
A cornfield.

How does your dog get into the house?
Through the labra-door!

What does it mean if you find a set of horse shoes?
A horse is walking around in his socks!

Why did the boy stand behind the horse?
He thought he might get a kick out of it.

What do you get from a forgetful cow?
Milk of amnesia.

What did the alien say to the plant?
"Take me to your weeder!"

If you had fifteen cows and five goats, what would you have?
Plenty of milk!

Patient: Doctor, I feel like a goat!
Doctor: Really? And how are the kids?

What do you call a sheep with no legs?
A cloud.

What do you get from a pampered cow?
Milk that's spoiled.

What do you call a
pig with three eyes?
A piiig.

Why did the
chicken run out
onto the basketball
court?
Because the referee
whistled for a fowl!

Young man, can you reach that package of beef from the top of the freezer?
No ma'am. The steaks are too high.

What do cows eat for breakfast?
Moosli!

What did the polite sheep say to his friend at the gate?
After ewe.

Have sheep ever flown?
No, but swine flu.

What did the duck say when she bought lipstick?
Put it on my bill!

FUN ON THE FARM

Why did the two pigs go to Las Vegas for their vacation?
To play on the slop machines.

How did the farmer find his lost sheep?
He tractor down.

Why does Santa have three gardens?
So he can hoe hoe hoe.

What do you call a cow with only his two left legs?
Lean beef.

When do you know it's time for a farmer's family to go to sleep?
When it's pasture bedtime.

What has five fingers and drives a tractor?
A farm hand.

What kind of animal goes OOM?
A cow walking backward!

What do you call a tale with a twist at the end?
A pigtail!

Why did the farmer think someone was spying on him?
There were moles all over his field.

A cross between a cocker spaniel and a poodle is a called a cockapoo. So what do you call a cross between a cockapoo and a poodle?
A cock-a-poodle-do!

What do you call a chicken crossing the road?
Poultry in motion.

How do hens dance?
Chick to chick!

What is the best way
to carve wood?
Whittle by whittle.

Why did the farmer
drive a steamroller over
his field?
He wanted to grow
mashed potatoes.

Why do male deer
need braces?
Because they have
buck teeth.

Why did the rooster get a tattoo?
He wanted to impress the chicks.

What do you get from an invisible cow?
Evaporated milk.

First cow in a field: Moo.
Second cow: Ohhh, I was going to say that!

Why did the ram run over the cliff?
He didn't see the ewe turn!

What was the result when two silkworms had a race?
It ended in a tie.

OUT TO SEA

Teacher: Who can tell me which sea creature eats its prey two at a time?
Pupil: Noah's shark!

What do sea captains tell their children at night?
Ferry tales.

Where do fish sleep?
On a waterbed!

Teacher: What musical instrument do Spanish fishermen play?
Cast-a-nets!

Why don't clams give to charity?
Because they're shellfish.

Teacher: Why was no one able to play cards on Noah's Ark?
Pupil: Because Noah stood on the deck!

What kind of noise makes an oyster grouchy?
A noisy noise annoys an oyster!

Teacher: Where do you find starfish?
Pupil: In the Galack Sea!

Where can you find an ocean with no water?
On a map.

Which beach item gets wetter the more it dries?
A towel.

What lies at the bottom of the ocean and shakes?
A nervous wreck.

Customer: Waiter, what's wrong with this fish?
Waiter: Long time, no sea.

What happened when the restless sleeper bought himself a waterbed?
He got seasick.

Lifeguard: You can't fish on this stretch of beach!
Boy with fishing rod: I'm not – I'm teaching my pet worm to swim.

What happened when the salmon went to Hollywood?
He became a starfish.

Why don't fish parents tell their children about electric eels?
They're just too shocking.

What music do they play in underwater nightclubs?
Sole music!

What did the passing seagull say to the pilot of the motorboat with no engine?
"How's it going?"

Which game is popular with fish?
Name That Tuna.

Which two fish can you wear on your feet?
A sole and an eel.

Did you hear about the two fish in a tank?
One was driving, and the other was manning the guns.

Wife: Doctor, is there any hope for my husband? He thinks he's a shipwreck.
Doctor: I'm afraid he's sunk, ma'am.

Why did the man go swimming in his best clothes?
He thought he needed a wet suit.

How do jellyfish police capture criminals?
In sting operations.

What did the walrus do after he read the sad book?
He started to blubber.

Watership Down

How can you tell that the ocean is feeling friendly?
It keeps waving at you.

Which fish once ruled Russia?
The tsar-dine.

How can you tell two octopuses are dating?
Because they walk along arm in arm in arm in arm in arm in arm in arm in arm!

What can you expect from a clever crab?
Snappy answers!

How could you give yourself an injury gathering shellfish?
You might pull a mussel.

How do fish go into business?
They start on a small scale.

OUT TO SEA

What day do fish hate?
Fry day.

Where do ocean scientists keep their coffee mugs?
On the continental shelf.

Where do fish keep their savings?
In the river bank!

What do you call a man floating up and down on the sea?
Bob.

What happened when the boat carrying red paint crashed into one carrying blue paint?
Both crews were marooned.

Who stole the soap from the bathtub?
A robber duckie.

Why are dolphins
smarter than humans?
Because they can train
humans to
stand by the side
of the pool and
throw them fish.

What is the
traditional anthem of
the pig navy?
"Oinkers Aweigh."

Why didn't the sea captain's radio work in rough seas?
It was on the wrong wavelength.

What kind of fish are useful in cold weather?
Skates.

What do sea monsters eat?
Fish and ships!

What's fluffy and green?
A seasick poodle.

Why did the crab cross the road?
To get to the other tide.

Where is the safest place to see a man-eating fish?
In a seafood restaurant.

What grades did the pirate get in school?
High seas.

Which salad ingredient is the most dangerous for ocean liners?
Iceberg lettuce.

Who held the baby octopus for ransom?
Squidnappers!

What's the best medicine for seasickness?
Vitamin sea.

What do you get if you cross a bad golfer and an outboard motor?
I'm not sure, but I bet it goes, "Putt, putt, putt, putt."

Which fish come out at night?
Starfish.

Who wins all the money at the undersea poker games?
Card sharks.

What happens if you cross an electric eel with a sponge?
You get a shock absorber.

Why do pirates have a hard time learning the alphabet?
Because they spend so long at "C".

Why do whales sing?
Because they can't talk!

How do you close an envelope underwater?
With a seal.

What runs and runs without ever getting out of breath?
A river.

What do the underwater police travel in?
Squid cars!

What sort of snacks can you buy on a Chinese boat?
Junk food!

How did Robinson Crusoe survive after his ship sank?
He found some soap and washed himself ashore.

Why wouldn't the sailor eat any fruitcake?
He was worried about dangerous currants.

What sort of boats do clever schoolchildren travel on?
Scholar-ships!

Which vegetables do pirates like best?
Aaaaartichokes.

What did the deep-sea diver yell when he got caught in seaweed?
"Kelp!"

What do you get if you meet a shark in the Arctic Ocean?
Frostbite.

What did Cinderella wear when she went diving?
Glass flippers.

Which sea
creature can also fly?
A pilot whale.

What do you call a gull that flies over a bay?
A bay-gull.

Why are goldfish orange?
The water makes them rusty.

Why did the surfer wear a baseball glove?
Because he wanted to catch a wave.

What do you call a delinquent octopus?
A crazy, mixed-up squid!

What is in the middle of a jellyfish?
A jellybutton.

How do you keep in touch with a fish?
You drop it a line.

What do whales like to chew?
Blubber gum.

How do fish get to school?
By octobus.

Why did the burglar buy a surfboard?
He wanted to start a crime wave!

Who is the
ocean's most
dangerous outlaw?
Billy the Squid.

Where do mermaids go to see movies?
The dive-in.

What did the fisherman say to the magician?
"Pick a cod, any cod."

How much sand would be in a hole two feet long, two feet
wide, and two feet deep?
None – holes are empty!

Why did Captain Hook cross the road?
To get to the second-hand store.

OUT TO SEA

What do you get when you cross a bee with a seagull?
A beagle.

How does a penguin feel when it is left all alone?
Ice-olated.

What can you put into a barrel full of water to make it lighter?
A hole.

What is the coldest animal in the sea?
The blue whale.

Why do sea lions
swim in salt water?
Because pepper
makes them
sneeze.

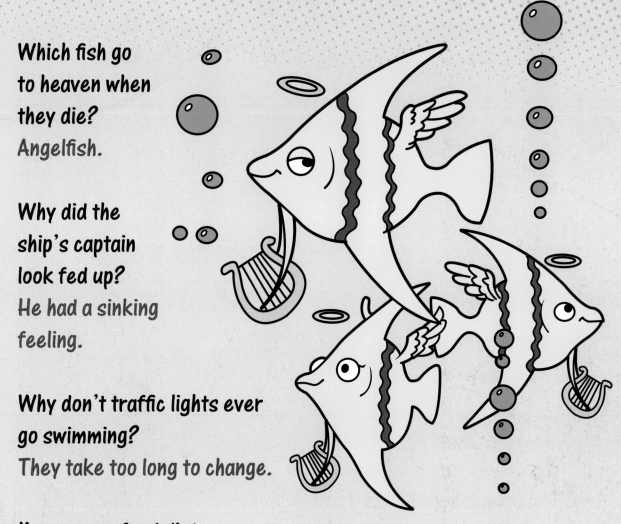

Which fish go
to heaven when
they die?
Angelfish.

Why did the
ship's captain
look fed up?
He had a sinking
feeling.

Why don't traffic lights ever
go swimming?
They take too long to change.

I'm on a seafood diet.
Are you losing weight?
No, because every time I see food, I eat it.

How did the dolphin make decisions?
It would flipper coin.

Who is the head of the underwater Mafia?
The codfather.

What kind of fish likes to eat between meals?
A snackerel.

What game do fish like to play at parties?
Tide and seek.

What did the pirate say to the woman in the shoe store?
"Where's my booties?"

What fish do knights like best?
Swordfish.

OUT TO SEA

How does a boat show affection?
It hugs the shore.

How do lighthouse keepers communicate with each other?
With shine language.

What can fly underwater?
A mosquito in a submarine.

What do you use to cut the ocean in half?
A seasaw.

Which fish are the best at home-improvement projects?
Hammerhead sharks.

Which fish works in a hospital? A plastic sturgeon.

What happens to a green rock when you throw it into the Red Sea? It gets wet.

What do you call a baby squid?
A little squirt.

Which sea creatures are the biggest cry babies?
Whales.

What's the best way to stuff a lobster?
Take it out for pizza and ice cream.